from ANIMAL

Ttoouli

C000095039

All rights reserved; no part of this book may be reproduced by any means without the publisher's permission.

ISBN: 978-1-913642-27-3

The author/s has asserted their right to be identified as the author of this Work in accordance with the Copyright, Designs and Patents Act 1988

Book designed by Aaron Kent

Edited by: Aaron Kent

Broken Sleep Books (2020)
Talgarreg,
Wales

Contents

Upcycling

from Animal Illicit

George Ttoouli

once something is no longer illicit,
punishable, pathologized, or used as
a lawful basis for raw discrimination
or acts of violence, that phenomenon
will no longer be able to represent or
deliver on subversion, the subcultural,
the underground, the fringe, in the same
way.

Maggie Nelson, *The Argonauts*

Composing

If i could just bring you back with love
then thought wouldn't be so painful

so many already instituted concepts, practices, and values are saturated with contempt
for the earth and the well being of its inhabitants.
—Lorraine Code

The white tail up   deer flees
from a train too far   perceives
rumble in the tussocks
perceives speed from and in
      the higher plane

i sit up   i train
my eyes down   track around
      receiveidentify
shape but not type in the turning
    a perhaps muntjac and fear
in the same motion in the same
deep grass

In this i'm sure there's wonder
the animal needs not
      consider: how sense
in neural networks
geopositions   eye and skull
        deer and train
passing   passing

Can i even remember what happened
without repainting the scene in brighter colours?

And if i could
    train without thought
      i would respond
    with love and only love
      to the deer that flees
        with its white tail up

Spider, missing

A poem in a notebook i've lost
about a spider in the garden i didn't see.
The cobweb threading in an autumn
made of cloudcast and leaf fall,
buddleia shedding into the weave.
The web stretched from ivy
to a plant that no longer exists
in this place, even by name. The site
extrudes absence, a plought plot
where vegetables might now grow.

The poem described the cobweb
as a university.
What did i mean by that?
The thought no longer exists
in the context between
ivy meninges and neural flora,
somewhere by this pathway.

And the term 'spiderdark'
compounds the memory of the poem,
an anti-spider, the hooked flora
where the lattice has unhooked
as if i've projected the image
of an image of a dream
into the space of an autumn
that never came around.

Somewhere in these pathways
which the wind tracks with its blown atoms,
atoms of leaf fall and cloudcast,
spiderdark and university, from lobe
to vegetable plot to ivy
i have budded the leylines
of a neurosis that never existed.

Badger, young, on the lawn

We had the lights down low, the fire on, when the lights came on.
Outside. Security. A badger, young, on the lawn, dancing,
jumping on things we couldn't fathom, running on, bounding again,
on mounds or something else. A pattern the night brought on.
Security. Like searching for a poem on a shelf filled with fictions
made of run-on sentences, we looked for something in each other which

on that night we might have found

but didn't. i'm in this room playing the scene through again. It happened
again. She moved on, i tried and now this second one is gone. i broke.
Couldn't hold together. i'm sorry. i'm like this badger looking in,
watching us wait for a poem from the lawn's auditorium. i can't grow,
i can't think why the badger won't leave, go on.

                            Go on. The lights aren't on,
the badger on the lawn left years ago and i want some sense from
what we did. Find none. i hope you're safe, your pattern's holding strong.
i've been holding shape out on the lawn since you've been gone.

At Northampton, riding north

the bridge before
      the station

to the right
      i saw a fox
         under the railway
           before the riverway
         in nettles and sunlight
    curling up
we passed before it settled

It was a foxlike fox, its fur an ember flavour
and the tail tip like it had been dipped
into just the right depth of paint—
you know what colour i mean, *think hard,*
there, that perfect image of a fox
you didn't think the world could hold.
How did those children's books
get their foxes right? You couldn't
do worse than go back to those books now
to see what a real fox looks like, could you?
             You might be tricked
into thinking, on

      an autumn evening,
        the sun fooling with the glaze
      on the meadow's grass

even the nettles growing over the rubble
look as glossy as a magazine's pages
everything tinted a better hue and how do
those glue mixers know what they're doing
to reality when they paste the pages with
a compound that turns photos into dreams?

They probably learned from watching
atmospherics on an autumn evening,
while riding north through Northampton
rail station, and for a moment, like us, forgot
what atrocities they'd commit
when they got home to the winter in their hearts.

suddenly
found myself
starting another
poem with suddenly
because i saw
two finches
in the birch
across from the office
and i don't even
remember why
no words came
but i stood
there doesn't even
matter where
this where
was or when
and no one
around to tell if
i was really better
as they burst into beautiful song
released that beautiful sound from their chests
that colour on the breast
i don't want to name
yes bursting out
of their beautiful
your beautiful
meaningless breasts
senseless beauties
and you had to
be there
to really know
why i'm
repeating myself
but whatever
it was
it's
gone

Meta

i used
to think
you had an
impossibly
long neck
so it
made perfect
sense when
you turned
into an
ostrich.

Men come
twice a week
to take
your eggs
and
one day
you'll be
nothing but
meat to them
your head
in the sand
neck for
the chopping

and one day
i'll be dead
my bones
ground down
to join
the desert
sand some
thing of
you still
buried in
me.

Gaia / a i a / Υγεια (also as Τεια

blue planet interspersed with green
and grey and desert yellow
where the light sits on it

      the mystery implies the root
      that also translates:
      health / earth / ear
      and sound implies a body
      which is also a system

          to be moving through
          to be recollecting you

      before one can be overthrown
      one must first climb above another's head

          remember: i didn't raise you up
          you climbed there yourself
          your startled spinning
          invites my own revolution—

the shadow i cast with this stance
is long enough to black out a planet

this one country alone (so many selves)
          i can't name but will call Greece
              despite --- ---- - ---- --- --- //

                                  alienness

daffodils clumped familiarly
    sprouted fear
knowing the treads
      will roll each year   over
      their heads   England   forever
cornered by terror
           who can tell
flower from rose?

    so bring me tulips
fleur-de-lis   bring hyacinth   damask
bring ginseng and ginger   cumin   cyclamen
and violets   bring their scents and pollen and seeds
    plant their stories in the meadows

          but March is out of sight
these daffodils plastic
      mouthing waxwork protest
the council sends its mower

  say it with a palpable design
    at some point our democracy resigned

untitled 26/8/17 (after midnight)

the garden's ragwort
proves the soil's richness
but what does this jaundiced horsekiller mean?

these past years i've buried meals in the garden
and been grateful for the company of bees

some respite for their horrors
online i've seen a Canadian farmer scoop fistfuls
from carpets of poisoned bodies. we are too.

our poison is money our language
murderous plosives: bayer
neonicotinoid
like a drone's rotor

but this poison
we've woven into breath
the map cuts into territory
we shouldn't have crossed

our garden lacks
other air

prove your point
and gasp

for Lee Harwood

love, my lungs don't work any more and i'm

    hey can you pass me that—

        open a window there's no

  and how long

      much longer

        ?

          —please?

Decomposing

this year a delayed heat

as if we'd all been holding back
until the temperature was right

now the trees are spurting green
abashed, even their ivy cladding

insufficient. April's thawed us out
and all the armour we'd built

around our minds has fallen off.
Where that leaves us: bare

bodies in the air in the ground
the ground riddled with tendrils

sucking our genes into the plants
the plants plucked for our selves

to ingest our selves. Abashed, even
when we're learning to forgive our

selves for our naked winters.

abashed April's armour
air abashed back

built bare
bodies cladding
delayed fallen

forgive green ground
ground genes
heat holding ivy

insufficient ingest
leaves learning minds
naked plants

plants plucked right
riddled spurting sucking selves
selves selves

temperature trees
thawed tendrils

winters
years

mutilated images

In Lefkosia i watched a cockroach
  walk beneath the barricade.

My battle scars unhealed
and the wounds began to ooze:
        a red dawn
on milky sands:
        Why so sour? What do you warn me of?
        What are you trying to say?

i write to try and close them:

        There was a man from Cyprus
        whose wounds were oozing pus.
                He lost his faith
                in nationhood.
        Is there something we need to discuss?

In Lefkosia i watched a cockroach
  crawl beneath the barricade.

Some images arrest you,
  take you out of the house
  hours before dawn
  into the street with a rifle to your head
  so you can mark the make
  on the barrel: MADE IN US

some images set fire to your homes
  and wait by the wells for the men

some images line the women in the street
  lift their skirts with bayonets
  and gut them when they protest

while other images take you into the dark
  between two huts and rape you
  and rape you again

and some images raise many questions
while some questions don't have any answers
and some images cannot be answered back to
and some images return to me mutilated

and some images return to me mutilated
and some images return to me mutilated

In Lefkosia i saw a cockroach
   reaching for a molotov.

No, that's not right.

In Lefkosia i socked a rock
   and swung it at a soldier.

In Lefkosia the crawl of progress
   crashes into barricades.

In Lefkosia i cocked a gun
   and breached the bloody barricade.

In Lefkosia the hotrod preachers
   speak of flaming hurricanes.

In Lefkosia the twilight sky
   wakes up to stark incendiaries.

In Lefkosia electric pylons
   fade into statistics.

In Lefkosia a dirty language
   crawls along the tenements.

In Lefkosia the UN line
   encroaches on our merriment.

In Lefkosia there's nothing holding
   insects to the barriers.

In Lefkosia they open fire
   on politician's motorcades.

In Lefkosia i threw my passport
  on the burning placards

What?   *What am i trying to say?*

In Lefkosia
          i watched a cockroach
                    crawl beneath
                              the barricades.

We see
not growth but
sudden cuts
a hedge, your hair

the grandchild's visits once a year
that lambasts the language we have—
      you've biggened he'd say to me

and the steadied hand that pulls
the jenga struts on welfare

until a thought occurs:
     when was it
last this bad?
     You match
the privet's long fronds
     with a year ago
and imagination grows insufficient

       ["quake island"   rose from the sea off Pakistan

                                   scientists   map
    the muddy mound's precise dimensions

       almost circular   175.7m on the long axis   160.0m
on the short axis   total area of 22,726 sq m

          sited near the town of Gwadar   after
    7.7-magnitude tremor
               intense shaking   disturbed
       stable sediments and gas at   sea floor,
                                          mud
volcano

          not expected to persist. The ocean will
    erode the soft sediments like it has with similar quake

islands in the past.

The Gwadar mound   fourth in the
region since 1945   third during the last 15 years.]

Not the birthed island
but the ocean cut into

the interrupted family when a child leaves
in any direction

(imagination is no space
for bringing objects together (and space

no place to stage a celebration
        (an open logic (erasure

            [

                        ever since the tsunami smashed into
        the Eastern Coast of Japan

                broke the concrete buildings that housed the
        reactor and caused radiation to leak into the atmosphere
                                    the radioactive contents
                        mix and spill into the sea water

                isotope of Caesium called 137Cs

            spreading freely across the ocean

                                            a heavy
        element   can make life sick

                            irradiated fish and
                        humans

recent maps   predict
          nearly all of the Pacific Ocean will have some
measurable amount of 137Cs related to the Fukushima
leak

          long term impact on life around the world.
This one accident in Japan could end up being one of the
worst ecological disasters in human history

                                        more a
question of WHEN rather than IF]

2/4/11 (unrecorded time)

late a
        gain
      an evening
                          rising   dirty
          water in the bucket   beside
          the algae-
                  filled pond

and a white
        tilt to orion's
              s
                    word   pointing
   east

                    but here we are
                                  west
          what
          ever   it means   to be
                                  west

                tending to the fires
                while the men hunt
                easterners

          things
                    like us
disappearing
          and a lizard bare
                            ly hidden

retreating
          under

                a rock from the blinding
          panopticon in the sky

bucket beside but be barely blinding
evening east ever easterners
late like lizard
orion's
water white word we west whatever west while

i am asking you if the birds flying through the bare branches of pedunculate oak in the late winter light caught in the long puddle in the woods where the path lies drowned are real.

And i am asking you if the birds in the sky where the light emits and the birds like shadows move against the branches of these oaks, which are like shadows – are they real?

And the birds in this poem? Are they a flock, are they black caps? Don't tell me they are a murder, not now.

i think i have got it wrong and that we are always getting it wrong and i don't think you have got it right.

weft of the high ropework in the deep sky
brings lights to the page

   should i believe a hazy thing
   waits in us to go badly?

     with ease we
     have weeds and beads

      but what do we see with our eyes
      that can abide with wisdom in us?

       with ooze
       woods and brood and bruise

        tell me you
        see in these words and birds
         what real is

8/10/13 15:10 Tocil Wood transect

decayed broken sycamore branch   dead leaf caught by the living

acorn cat   a   strophe   s through the oak   the den   t its boun   ty set s in
to litt er ear the though t   of soun d   tranquillised tranquillity

drift   be ached be ech   wood mud stuck

i vy   s naps   but does not sever sound ly

root syst   em expose d and shoe s cuf fed

moss over   take s th   e dead sap   ling in   to un death

future disaster in the wood pile : a lightning volley   the lighter fluid
brought by bored boys : beetle flambé : system unravelled

b rook's eros ion scrap es a bank mud trap   fis sures ex foli   ate the
ear th

tree s   tump how much can you   off er de   spite?

map a desp   e rate chaf fing at   my app roach

feat hers sug gest a tor n tai l : wing s till   on   the g round   off
ering to som et hing

you've been in woods : what you sawn? : i sawn a fallen tree : clean
separated isometry

bro   ken pav ing sla bs he avily dis loc ated

su nli ght s iz zl in g int o pho tos yn the sis   bro wn   spo ts of
pos   t r ain

   what trees were here in this glade   *and where have they gone?*

some thing fell too close to me and nearly shook me loose :
catastrophe sounds too much like hope collapsing and turning
through the canopy   who hurls these things at my heart and head?
when will their bolts stick again?

fens shrivelled before i got here still feel like my fault but this path
is not   it is a long time coming into my ken and the feet that i follow
are permission to keep making mistakes we should have corrected
by now

the cobw eb i wal ked thro ugh : sor ry spide r yo u 've ha d to
o much t im e a lone and t his new comp any crash es thro ugh y
our hous e

be rry foo tc ru shed a b loods po t a cyc le no circ le   w here cymb
als ag gre gate

dead s talks whi   te the g   round   with acci dental net   wor   ks
commun ic   ate ants f rom sour ce to h ome : dam age is a way
& no things m our n

i'm cash   ing in this im   age against the possibility   of
gales tear   ing down   the fore st's tall   est   tr   ees all i can see
is the for   est   giving s helter   eve n in   this im   agined dis
aster

road sp lits mood   in two pret ending s afe ty   does this
im   ply the wo od land's d   anger? A danger of wor ds what is   sp lit
betwe en wo odl   and and fo rest? dam aged im age

an oasis of horror

Death, the fertile region where we sought refuge:
flowers blossom out of the decayed bodies;
the bodies are flowers; the bodies are exhausted;
birds attend the water, drink the dead cells
we are made of. They do not care. The birds
are the dictators of my heart. The birds
are the executioners of absence in my heart.
My heart is made of birds, which is better than love.

                              absence attend

              blossom bodies

                                          bodies bodies

            birds birds birds

                                              birds better

cells care

                                          death decayed

              drink dead dictators

                  exhausted executioners

                                    fertile flowers
                              flowers heart

                heart heart
                    love made

                    made region

                          refuge
                  sought water

i have to admit and you've probably guessed by now
that much of this material is is coming from a fairly emotional place
and there's a lot of a lot of a lot of sorrow
but sometimes you you you know how it go it go it goes
when there's this catastrophe bearing onto onto
onto me and it starts to feel like everything i i s-s-see
is out of my control and i start to take it person-person-personal
ly and i just hope you're doing something for yourself
to make this problem go away
but sometimes there's just something you have something
        you just have to- have to s—
have to s have to s s s

oh fuck you poetry is there nothing you'll leave sacred nothing
        you won't taint

        you   you you
you've pulled my teeth for gemstones and cut out the tusk of my tongue
        and poured your superheated water down my throat
left a lake of arsenic in my guts
pumped the marrow from my limbs   and torn my digits for trophies
        fracked my ribs and pulled the fragments for paving
flushed my heart with cyanide looking for gold to make your trinkets
        and is it a wonder my heart still beats amid your poison
is it a wonder my arms still reach up to comfort you and hold you tight

        but i can't   i can't
           can't tell you   i can't tell you
                                       anything
     anything
           will be   all right

@

1/10/13 15:47 field observation with quadrat (rear of engineering building)

pink spray of meadow flower   tall thin green stems   give way to
brown seed heads   bulbous   worn stubble emerging   grass leaf
perpetrates   pale green with dark   dandelion   low amid wider
leafweed   tri-form and a dry spray   six inches high at most
curved by seeds   formed along top   multiple branches from
main stem   flowers   between decay states   fading to orange
lower petals falling along dock leaf   like dandelion   age denoted
by brown dotting   below grass layer   dry bracken   beneath
small blades barely two-millimetre widths   spike thin   then
earth a healthy drydogshitbrown   within pink flowers   small
stamen curl up   darker pink fingers   cup claws surround   paler
pink fronds   at heart

age along amid
barely below
beneath between blades
bracken branches brown

brown bulbous claws
cup curl
curved dandelion
dandelion dark
darker decay denoted

dock dotting dry dry drydogshitbrown
earth emerging fading falling

fingers flower flowers
flowers formed
fronds give grass grass green green heads heads

Mona Lisa

healthy heart high inches
layer leaf leaf leafweed low
lower main meadow

millimetre most multiple

orange pale paler
perpetrates petals pink pink pink
pink seed
seeds six

small small spike spray
spray stamen states stem
stems stubble surround tall thin
thin top tri-form two way

wider width worn

Something hurtling across the woods, which you try to record

if I were a swift cloud to fly with thee
—PB Shelley

Positioned by the hundreds of paces
the mics taut pockets of range
at clearings among the sycamores,
porous barriers within which speech
recedes. The birds launched vectors
at the recording transect by months
and he waited in all rains and suns
every range of weather pockets and
whatever else the climate pitched
between that summer and into autumn.

ossif[ied]   eons [and]   soft aces
[if] spears   [s]ought   poets'   orange
alea[tory]   song the sigh   [of] amours
poor harrier   sin   which   spe-[ech]
ci[ti]es   etherise   haunched   seconds
[b]ather   orange   eyes   moan
an eu[logy] way   e[v]en arraigned   ones
veer in [o]range   heath poet   [sou]nd-
hover   [silently]   [   ]
e[v/']en   [a]   humming [bird]   an i[ota of] awe

And then one day the vector catches
to a perfect coincide; the bird launches
along the path of the recorders
and the song takes off just at the metre
of the third microphone. What wonder!
Between the third and fourth you hear
her trill fading just briefly into the sky's
ambience then returning as she reaches
the next node in you: transect. How much
have you earned in so brief a life?

Ossified eons land their soft paces
as spears which seek the poet's ranging,

aleatory song. The sigh of amorous
poor harriers, in which species
etherise their haunched seconds
at the orator's eyes, and morning
is an eulogy, a way of evening arraigned once
verse inaugurates the angels' heathen poetry.
Windhover silence   [here again]
this even humming bears an iamb of awe.

Sussex Envoi

The Sussex sea slows, slower, then ceases to drape
the once hard stones with its breakers, the expression
of the pebbles now one fine-smoothed crescent bowing
of bay-stretched sand. Ripples freeze in the red-orange
sunlight, a water-walked pathway, set in a wax-
soft texture. Two pairs of eyes take visionary
skates across the immutable blaze. Together
our lips find ways to sing the dawn into silence.

*

ways sing   silence lips   find dawn
together skates   immutable   blaze across
visionary   two texture   take soft   pairs eyes
wax water   walked sunlight   set pathway
stretched sand ripples   red orange freeze   bay
smoothed pebbles   fine crescent bowing
stones once hard   expression breakers
slower   slows   sea   drape   ceases

*

ceases   drape sea   slows slower
breakers   expression hard   once stones
bowing crescent   fine   pebbles smoothed
bay freeze   orange red   ripples sand stretched
pathway set   sunlight walked   water wax
eyes pairs   soft take texture two   visionary
across blaze   immutable skates   together
dawn find lips   silence sing ways

◊◊◊◊ ◊◊◊◊ ◊◊◊◊ ◊◊◊◊ ◊◊◊◊ ◊◊◊◊ ◊◊◊◊ ◊◊◊◊ ◊◊◊◊ ◊◊◊◊ ◊◊◊◊ ◊◊◊◊ ◊◊◊◊ ◊◊◊◊

Recycling

preface

i don't want to inflect these poems for you with too much of myself at least that part of my self which the poetry doesn't automatically allow to pass through its gates but there's no doubt there's an atmosphere of sadness in these pages one i should acknowledge one you can't have missed it's been a really hard year for me and the more human i try to feel in language the less human i want to be not like death but transformation like what John Baker wanted to erase in him self so as to approach the peregrine that absence of an outline that absence of things that make us human and maybe that's what Eliot meant about wanting to escape emotion and maybe that needs a kind of language that doesn't call itself poetry tunes out from rhythm from performance and if i let the words out of my control and pass them over to the birds entirely i might manage to escape myself

tweee tweeeeeeee twih twi-oo
tweee tweeeeeeee twih twih twih twih twih
tweee tweeeeeeee twih twi-oo

feetfall

Calm chuck orkut clackt. Mesh shutter grit.
Ort. Rut rubble. Ick. De-pat. Hush. Ortik. Grist.
Poured down. Crit. Percale. Tonk wrong. Sproing
ordnance. Stored long borehole. Cort. Bored. Long
boing. Drop polyp. Hill up. Clod cop. Oak lip. Crisp
lick. Hello. Soft spring. (crumping scoosh oft hunk bekist)
Crab crab scarb crave stag. Tong. Og. Dog. (cricket
ticket) sog. Report blag. Snort. Talk. Flick. Whisp.
Err. Alert sharp aspect. Feet odd. Leeward. Eaten.

At the crux of four tracks, two leaflittered, but
the wider junctures soiled. Where are the seasons' wide-eyed
signs? By expo-/era- sure, gone. Calm chucked
orkut of the cort-stepping. The oak-lips' crisp lick,
the bridges oft-sprung boards drop polyps at hill
cups. Black bracken earth eschews root digits.
Trees which split twenty feet up, while others fork
at a child's height. Trauma, love, coextensive.

Scientists no longer believe the green sea
snail can take on the properties of photosynthetic
plant cells when they eat them. Instead
like a camel, it digests these cells over months
even in darkness subsisting on thought alone.

Synthesis is a kind of coming together.

The sea snail's synthesis is synthetic.

To be synthetic is to say i am not really in love.

Is synthesis a kind of theft or a kind of eating?

If you eat this poem it tastes of snapshots.

        sis, the sins
   we've committed don't even scratch
      this poem's
          crazy thesis

<<wanted to say something here
about the house martins that scrib
about the balcony every day and hurl
their "broken continuities" at the cats
at lunchtime as if they really want you
to know there's something getting on
their wicks, their collective wicks
and how my eye's (eyes are!) really drawn
to that flash of orange on their underwings
and their cruciform outlines apart
from their forked tails seem swiftly
and how my eyes (eyes!) are really drawn
on right now and i'm asleep all lowercase
hours but really i can't do it i can't at all
there's no one to write this for / you
are / writing it / for every one / and any
way my brother says they're swallows
if they've orange flashes and black hoods>>

["broken continuities" taken from a line in Robin Blaser's 'that cat', in reference to
Haydn being interrupted, the phrase italicised to imply quotation, but i can't be
bothered to source it accurately myself, i just like the way it sits.]

🐁☼🁢☺🐦☠

At the Natural History Museum

The spinal juts evolve along the line
the soft sounds grow into chunks and blocks
of shape and the shapes rectangularise;
the daggers of the spine are now like people.
Plunicorns and lynx tips, displays of colour, expanded
vermilion having terminations on cubital waxwings
the light drawn in and sent back beautiful.

      Instinct sends us back to things we know are safe.
      If a refuge does us harm, but creates emotional security,
      even so, we return to it. Addiction and instinct are related.

there is no country which has now any
attraction for us, without it is seen   April May 1836,
right astern, & the more distant &   Mauritius,
indistinct the better. We are all utterly home sick.   Charles Darwin

Slowly and by little starts the mountains rise,
the chain emerging from the mud of sea bed
           linking species to species.

      the two-shelled creature in my head, my brains
         the two shelled creature in my chest, my lungs
           preserve these, their history is multitude

      Not the process but the feel
      of petrified wood attracts me. i
      haven't a language for history.

The mind is a chaos of delight   Charles Darwin on seeing
               rainforest for the first time

      the lizard lies limp, back peeling
      and toes slack on the branch,
      a length of tail
      casual between twig spines,
      the long slow change

of greens and greys
the wood thrown clothing
over the floor
a broom of leaving in the air
eyes slain into sleep and breathing
a plume of bronchia
skeins of dessicant yesterskin;
once I was awake, but now...

I think that you will humanize me, & soon
teach me there is greater happiness,
than building theories & accumulating
facts in silence and solitude.

20th January 1839,
letter from Charles Darwin
to Emma Wedgwood

the unity of type of the great changes in embryo *the hand to clasp, the bat's wing to fly... the porpoise to swim,* the skeletal design shared with all.

The lock and key of orchids and their pollinators, the perfect beauty of this symbiosis is astonishing to me. Why does a species adapt itself almost in service to another species? Why evolve to this degree of dependency? It feels almost as if strength can be drawn from this ability to interconnect. But where is the strength here? How do delicate orchids flourish by this web?

Orchids must be a demonstration of the power of complex systems, in a microcosm. Variation is key. At points of threatened survival the genetic code seems to shift - no doubt over millions of years. Or shorter but expansive periods. The point is to go on fucking.

9/8/12 11:50-13:50

after Larry Eigner

this happened hours
  ago
  why
   tell
    you
     now

  dogs
large & small
children

 barking

 is the lawn
  is a mower
a vacuum
  cleaner a
   strimmer
    or why

    nasal plane
     cuts through

can't hear
 selfbreath
in or dinate drone
     rone
      rone

laught
 er of dogs
or yelp
 ing of

   child
 all simultane accrues
  bright wild

even an order
order an even

if this happened
hours ago
own-lie-i   impose
super   impose
no i-amb   ient or envi
iron
ment

but sim   ul   tan   acrum   eous

where systems
bite each the other
child mower lawn dog
strimmer plane breath

this is how much i love
loved   you
this is how much
i want to be under
(stood)

A Note on Process

close your eyes and focus on your breathing

breathe in   breathe out   breathe in   breathe out

relax your bladder, but not too much

breathe in   breathe out

You are in a bright field on a summer's day. The sun is warm and the bees are buzzing nearby, but not so much that you are worried about being stung.

You are enveloped in the warm sun and you slowly slowly slowly   slowly   slowly   drift into sleep in the shade of a hedge.

When you wake up –

don't open your eyes, breathe in   breathe out

– it is night, and a nearby jasmine bush calms the air about you with its perfume. You are floating in a cloud of sweet marzipan and your hay fever is mysteriously gone.

You take one   long   deep   breath

drawing the scent into your lungs

and breathe out   and again   breathe in –

This time, as you inhale, your consciousness travels into your body with the scent. You are rushing into your nasal passages, through pipes and fleshy tubes, down towards the oesophagus

and breathe out

You breathe in again, deeper still. You are a speck of pollen – *information added to matter!* – rushing into your nostrils, down through your oesophagus, into the bronchial passages, where you linger, weightless in the red dark

and breathe out

And you take another even deeper breath, speeding without inertia through mucal canals, the warm red dark of the throat and the bronchial tubes, then burst into the wide cavern of your left lung – the wrong one? – floating above a vast meadow of twinkling tunnel mouths, your alveoli, glistening with mucus.

You float gently, weightless, your consciousness free of fear, free of desire, free of all the worries in your life, including whether you left the soup boiling on the stove before you began, or whether the planet is about to burn up.

You are a weightless speck of pollen in your right lung – *no, left!* – a molecule of scent. You roll with the energy of unseen forces onto your back and float downwards, settling with a small fleshy spring on the top of a giant cilium, which is now scaled to the size of a hillock beneath you. Only the open space of your lung above you, walls inflating and deflating to the thrub of your heart beat in a distant chamber, means anything.

With the speed of the miniscule you slide into an alveolus and evaporate through the membrane into the warm pace of a capillary's flow. You are a speck of consciousness in your own blood. With every boom of the heart, you are thrust into the incoherent rushing of tubes. You ebb through the red pipes of your body's funnels and sphincters, the warm traffic of corpuscles and platelets nothing more than a brush stroke on your awareness.

You thrust at lightspeed through the chambers of your heart, a sad, rusting boiler room, crushed and uncrushed, and you scud through the aorta and down into the arteries of your bowels.

A strange thrust sideways and you are in your left kidney being drawn towards a tall net of fleshy gauze, through which you are filtered, the membrane passing through your consciousness, your consciousness passing through your kidney's filters, then down through a tube, into the broad, stretched sphere of your bladder, the curved walls rubberish and marbled with the irregular lines of stretched wrinkles.

With a flush you are dashed down, through the puckered muscle at the base of your bladder and through your narrow urethra, towards an approaching yellow light.

You emerge into the daylight of your stream, an ochre shower. Your humanity is clean, your thoughts, worries, your consciousness, all purged away.

You have only the animal of your body left. You are pure, with nothing but the fading warmth of your passing and the scent of foxes on a doorstep.

Cerealisation

"Organic farmers grow
their crops without chemical
pesticides and fertilizers, keeping
the soil fertile and nutritious.
Crops are left to breathe and given
plenty of room to grow, meaning
ingredients are naturally
nurtured from seeding to
                   cereal bowl."

Jordan's Organic Porridge Oats (750g)

~

Organic farts grow
their cross-examinations without cherub
petrochemicals and fetlocks, keeping
the solecism fertile and nutritious.
Cross-examinations are legation to breathe and given
plenty of rosary to grow, mechanic
initials are naturally
nurtured from seeding to
            cervix boxroom.

~

Organic fasteners grow
their crotchets without chicanery,
phalluses and fiascos, keeping
the soloist fertile and nutritious.
Crotchets are lemming to breathe and given
plenty of rotation to grow, medic
inks are naturally
nurtured from seeding to
            chain-smoker bracket.

~

Crops naturally nurtured
to and from, to and from
seeding chemical
pesticides
breathe into rooms.

Crops, meaning
ingredients,
are leftist fertilizers,
are fertile bowls
without Organic growbags,

keeping the soil
and given plenty of cereal
grow their farmers nutritiously.

~

It saw the harvester does his collections without chemical insecticides and
the fertilizer of the nutrition and counts on basic fruitful and that one. The
collections are left, the end to breathe and the abundance, of which the
video of the section is injection, in the order are developed that, meaning
the component, consolidated he naturally with Müslischüssel.

~

Ecologic skis, landmined durkas,
endear a greedier udder. Kamikaze skiers
pesticide Roget's stunned god, while ninjas hold a
jolly den of fruit bars over ice rinks.
Even greedier the overlaid checkout tills
that track vegetable rats, over days
massed with plates. Toiled vocals will cut foetid errors,
ingratiate dying serums in natural light,
pledges freezing on until
corn screams.

~

May he pollute my jaunty stoat with cassava.
Unending culture, riding ill mothers, keeps millionaires still.
Pesticide de ja vu: it is testy, hides
mouldy villains, casting total evil,
polluting culture, was a cool hinge at a jaunty
pail. Cassava rooms, *amis,* the end dabbed
by an inedible lunatic, slit into cults,
rickets-stabbed all at once. Culverts
terrify villains with cassis.

~

Female worms organise in the tofu.
You knit daubed herbs, smeared egos
plainly laid dire by agues re-tithing God's ewe,
while prides of withered lions marathon
knitted cauls and you godly anaemics in cowls
digging lines of difficult sins. Golly!
Sunk wisdom is nature's oil
made thin – oh, if only i had
grown forwards, poor lentils.

the river's full of a minereal chatter
and ~~house martins~~ swallows scrib and munerate tombforms
through noonlight insect pursuits. the avocado
branches catch rangepitched cockerel and goat
tangling out of expected resounds.
just beyond the balcony's possessive everything
a blank green preening in the winding air.
i'm utterly winded by distance : love of voices
sends me wombwards, a strip of whitecaps
at both ends of vision :
                  sea mountain
          breaker crests   ridge path finder
       far sudden   port-transed
     being between two and sitesighted

cba

Reading Maximus

All of this actually happens without / linebreaks but i'll add them later.
And i'm pleased
      (to say i get Olson's use
      of parentheses
      better than he does now
      is an understatement / *aggrandizement* (but
don't forget the last thought you had could just leave you
well

                                  hung

~

               [   ]
               [   ]
               [   ]
               [   ]
               [   ] *

~

Dinner by the lake
tastes of
the memory of dinner
by the lake

      Oh yeah, all you people reading
      don't you think / don't you think
      you should be reading something
      ELSE. But hey, look, a rhyme
      to keep you from checking the (rag)time.

                                              *readers are invited
                                            to draw their own
                                            spiral glyph in the
                                            space provided*

for Maggie O'Sullivan

tongues dipping in things
       in wounds in tins of red paint
in in in trees in nectar in air
       in commons in dipping in governments
in tongues tongues dipping in language
       tongues licking up lakes and leaving valleys
feathers scullery maids bus tickets
       lactic plastic and exceptions and industries
tongues leaving fingerprints on chickens
       on malted bread on chickens eating
malted bread in barns with a fine marmalade
       made of soy and wine and made of marriages
and mortgages and miscarriages made of chicken bones
       and the bones of tongues the bones
of prose the bones of promises
       of children playing board games playing war games
with daisy chains or red paint tins or bombs or their real tongues

17/8/16 14:40 Swanswell Park

stopped en route to the health centre looking at a young swan and the phrase popped into my head

   the young swans look like

hunted for something witty to add: *drunk punks / ruffled rocks / feathered footballs.* Energy is all in the language and in wanting to make you smile

but nothing sat right: the cygnets were half the size of adults, a messy grey, swimming with the awkward agency of their immaturity and looking *just like themselves.*

but reminded me of something : of myself : of the same teenage gangling the discomfort and urge to stretch out of the clothes i was always outgrowing that feeling you're an odd one out in any group like a young swan only it is its own self and it had taken me so long to remember because i have forgotten what i is and i don't know if i want to be another I

this is the stage before reinvention when the down hasn't dropped off and the whiteness of adulthood's rules and rigour approaches but for now the bird is at its most meaningless as totally a self and totally an other as it can be : the breeze works the surface of the swans' well into visual music

                    a somewhere else all
          ready thinking the swell's wan
                    ob-/sub- / sub-/ob- / -ject

Upcycling

Bat

And i imagine a bat
                        falls into my lap
a folded pocket

            with no desire
clumsy, lost, trusting

in time to be caught
                        and it looks up
through its drawn wings and asks for nothing

though i expect it to speak
                                i expect the night
to speak
            to the strange corners of the veranda
or my mind, which are the same
                                stage
                        on which the bat and i
perform
            in something we don't recognise

is still a language
                        which says: i need you

i need you
            because love   because love

                                    has folded
love folded
                itself around
                            around me
and this stillness
                        this stillness

has nothing   nothing

for us
        for our love

if trees broadcast data
   in leaf packets   insect bites
            the edges of messages
not corruption   integrated information

as fingerspaces   gaps between branches
   exchanging letters on air
among all gaps   bodies   including ours
   a squirrel's chatter
         distorts into spaces
      the body secure
            in a sycamore's apex

sunlight coats our arms with words
in the shape of molecules   skin writes back
a reflection of colour   gratitude
            on the soft surface of light

            everything means
as if there was never an otherwise
for excluding anything from our hearts
name-calling anything unintelligible
         incapable of language
but our own shortcomings: what
have we learned to see in connections?

corruption
                     is impossible
   safety   unsafety   extremes of
                              imagination
the same lacunae   different meanings
         for each of us

corruption   impossible
            ideals   non-entities
nothing is real but the communication
itself   equals a whole impartial fact
   im   part   ed
                  bread crumbs
                     recording the path

a broken trunk   an epiphany meeting
    epiphanies   the junction   between
                          understanding   and   awe

    like lea ping   betw een   bran ches
                 sa   fety   un   sa   fety

as if   (no) know   ledge (edge)   is light
    (light) ning   stri k in g   it   sel f

cherries
saturday 20th july 2013, late afternoon,
for simon turner

Walking from home to the bar on campus with Simon, we found ourselves stepping on cherry stones. Not "the hearts of atheists" as he once put it, but the real stuff, and we looked up and the trees were big as limes (that's an exaggeration) and there were several of them between the flats and the urban through-route, red spotting the green leaves, green pasting the beige bricks.

i pulled down a branch, wondering who owned them. He thought they'd be rife with the exhausts, but we picked two and they were a deep colour you could lose things in, or find things and we ate them and they were sweeter than we expected.

On Tuesday i saw a couple as i cycled home pulling down the branches to taste the fruit. One was wearing cargo shorts and the other Lycra leggings and i'm saying that not because it is important but because i want you to think about what that means to you and what kind of image it brings into your mind.

On Thursday several people clustered under each tree, pulling down the branches and harvesting the fruit, gathering what they could in their pockets, or using teamwork to load up piles of cherries in their pouched sweatshirts. i nearly bumped into a man carrying a ladder as i walked by and it was a very specifically rustic ladder.

By Friday the street was rammed with bodies, the trees torn, traffic queuing and howling, debris and fistfights smearing the road, people crabbing over each other to climb to the top of the body pile, children chewing the bark and babies crawling along the pavement, trampled, their faces drooling a red juice, picking the stones from the ground and sucking them for the last drop of taste, the air symphonic with groaning and dying. A starving postie clutched at my ankle, pulled herself out of a pile of stones and tried to bite my bollocks off.

Some of this actually happened, but, as a metaphor, all of it is happening right now in the world as you read this, or because you are reading. The difference between a metaphor and an animal. The difference between us and animals. The difference between an end stop and the little words that join us to the world. When i hold up a mirror, i am covering myself with a veil, coating my tongue in silver until the last cherry tastes of myself.

'She has developed her own alphabet'
for Chloe Fremantle

imbued with the beauty of being somewhere
closer to a particular reality
aerial view of what the plan
homage to the tree / vast and extraordinary
black pines as old as that
some of these little studies
some of these wilder landscapes /
French landscapes
move on to something different
out of people / at the end / part of that
why don't you paint about it?
a vast expansive / inviting house
something about the skies / would fit in here
part of an ongoing / October
something much more urban / in the everyday
industrial / fantastic big skies
how light affects things on one level
even in the industrial / love can give you
summers in Scotland
a lot of black / three-dimensional things
express something about / we're all going
to experience / my parents loved gardening
all the plants were extra friends
respond more to gardens
terribly it had been / a very small garden
oasis you go into / energy and nourishment you go into
hide what things are from
the same patterns recur / back very much
to say before we move / much better than
the radio on the fifth / perception – colour –
understand why light / our brain interprets
transposes because of the light / in our minds
quality of light / lit by / a huge effect
talk about colour constancy / a key to our survival
a red mushroom / knows it's dangerous / to bright
pink and pale green / keep constant the colours
to survive if it gets / made—

to respond to natural light / at times
i think you'll notice / geographically / the size of France
the softness is richer and different / colours we want –
to have / inside us / picking up things in the atmosphere
forgotten things in the market
in different places / really the palette
thin and like a wash
splash of something down / happier with matter
smear them all over you / exposed to the
Park in a lovely old church hall
allergic from / – O Lord! – / all sorts of things
heavier with it / all kinds of things with it
water-based / the side of the drive / we discussed
the thirties / early / obviously there's / instinct
clinical / might do / walking backwards and forwards
painting not just the form but the
                                        extraordinariness

sock monsters

Eleventh of February, year of—oh emm gawd!—twentieth and sixteen
for JSL on the anniversary of his birth-date

Cher M. L—,

Hopping or strolling downhill near where you live
and everything normal, the headphones in your ears
asking *why'd you leave the keys upon the*—
and the wild park's green—
                    before the dual carriageway
          which has six lanes at the roundabout—
green and the brook under the road
          a step happens then between world and sea
biome and bubble, no reason, a jump

                    cut to the Pacific floor where a herd of socks
                    mismatches across the bedrock floor
                    discarded before you went out into the day's currents.

          Let's say breath is a protected space
an imaginative zone encased in a plastic ball
bearing the pressure of a mile of ocean above

                    This is mythic—no, EPIC!—The lights
                    off, camera
                              ghosts
                                        the flock of sock
                    monsters known as Xenoturbella
                    alien footholders, millennarians
                    old feetwarmers, muscled moutharses

          —the directorial cue, the music:
                    John Luther Adams' apocalyptic orchestra
          the *seenic vous*! alert the surtitles

Just beyond the Attenborough voiceover
  you hear traffic washing tarmac
    the carriageway's alienable current
  and a Singaporean poet mumbling,
                    Why you no tidy your room, la?
then the submersible gangles out of the fire station bay

at the roundabout's opposite side
where the dark glum undersea swallows perception
and with transparent cylindrical arms
vacuums each ancient fleshbag
the whole herd of purple socks
into its technowomb

But Alvin, they're so safe here,
they have a functional anarchy!

(But the subpoetmarine is
nobody's double)

Xenoturbella exists outside of h u m a n t i m e !

(Beat. Laughter.)

This is where we came from!

(Silence.   SILENCE!)

A Midlands rain cuts in, drowning poets
and the submersible's six propulsion hums,
the Pacific's gravelly heaving and communal grind,
the washing petrol on the roads

a heavy rain
made of brown clumps of algae swollen to death
with ferrous sulphates, fat from sucking sea-oh!-too
sick geoengineering solved by rogue geoengineering
this ungineered Geo now trying to explain to you

A   a f
v   c   i s   f   a
e   d   e   t   t i
c   o
n

Lightning storm at sea seen from Meskla, 22 September 2016 around 22:00, recollected 14/10/16 – 16/10/16 with interjecting thoughts

Not knowing where to begin

                        doesn't mean

don't begin but get going   so many things

i could be doing   you

might say the words can't be taken   right

out of some poor mug's gob

but the breath can be stolen   (am i rite?)

and words swept into a droughted place

without permission or punctuation   just because

a person's lungs have been so full   their voice

freely cast across uninhabited valleys   like one day

one day, let's say, the breath goes out all at once

never comes back   they know what they've lost

and say, loudly, fuck all those others   OTHERS

they've lived   lived without   breath   (she's slowing now)

without breath for their whole lives   what is it?

What is it to then have less air

  in   out   in   in   subs tract a tion tus :   i wanted

to say something against lightning and love   to strike

out that adage of being in love   —   you know what,

we were on the roof and the stars marshalled

up a fleet of stories and symbols   gunshots

flared over the ridge and more flashes we came to see

as storm : that : *that* : love was   witnessing

being left breathless, incomprehensible   carrying words

i had no air then   for you i found some

would spend the last breathable

composition   i watched a NASA video of carbon mono-

and di-oxide releases across a single breathable year

the colours were   breath taking

like watching a clear plastic bag   drawn down slow

finding a child's blue body centred in a room

you only left for a few thousand years to go wrong

come back to nothing left to breathe

                                                % N2
                                                % O2
                                                % CO2
                                                % NO2
                                                % S
all of it is toxic   outside of a narrow margin
permission to speak   parts per million   freely denied
something whispered in the gaps   between   in
out in in (sub tract us) substrate   what air
do rocks need to live?   i listened
to a short film narrated by George Monbiot about the wolves
of Yellowstone   seeing what happened
          when you removed the deer   how they changed
the rivers, the whole system   "tropic shifts"   imagine

          what would happen
                        if you removed the humans
no one struck by lightning   or love   no one
to write you love   letters   no one to read my words
when there's no air to breathe with
and all these words   it's so easy to forget
love is the whole storm   not the bolt
          near   far   it doesn't matter
as long as there's breath   the whole duration of it
and us   let's try not   to be terrified
          of everything   but each other

                                                                    ∞

[petrograms]

HAY'S
A MAIZE BLAZED
BLAYS A MAZING
ZE
HA

FURS
FURZE
CURSIVE
VURZE

EYES BELIE
PREYES
LY
RE

PRAIRIE
FOR THE
AIRY
RIE
FAE

BREEZE
PLEASES
   SNEAZES

   STEP
   PING
   ING
   IN

   UNF
       FARE
   AIR
P R A Y E R
FOR FAIR AIR

   GNAW
   MORE
   ORES

∞

HOURS
FORM FROM
YOUR OURS

NO NEWS
FUSING
EWES

FIERY
PRIORY
EYRIE

FRIEZE
GRIEVES
AG
GRIEVIOUS
VES
EA

9/10/14 16:00 – walking Tocil Wood, from lakes to Meadow

Absolutely sun falling to the lakebed
everything fowl swims the lit air
ground guzzlers, throat chuckling.

Berry dead stretcher postmortal beam
  piles birth hazard economics
 spike day binge strobes
    nut harvest palm-to-trunk
dizzy overheads   radicle gouge
   fungal knots—mosquito mestizo
waltz to air's aria   surface attuned
   attenuated tension—fungal knots afford
fire pile pyramids beetled budder

Berry postmort(em): beam-piles birth binges palm-to-trunk
    pyramids beetled buddlier postmort(al).

imagine / every name we share is precise

from a line by Stephen Cope
for Florence Sunnen

i'm dismantling myself, part by part
to give to you: the birds i imagine
in my heart and the bars that hold them;
the song itself now yours and the strings
condemned to play this off-time key.

A dolphin leaps an amphibrach
between my skull and liver
when you listen to me, transforms
from turtle to tortoise and back again.

Every limb is a deertrack rambling astray
in fern and shrub, the long meadow returns
to me as skinfurze, now yours,
every pitted and permitted surface of my outside,
microbes rewriting communal epics in my pores.

Reach out and take up these words
and strike them how you will, out or through—clouds
of mosquitoes at dusk; shoals, herds
at the trough of my self orating
everything i give you when i give.

fern leaps limb
      listen liver long
            off-time orating outside
                  rambling reach returns rewriting epics
                        everything now clouds
                              communal condemned epics
                              everything

            self shoals shrub skinfurze
                skull song strike strings
                    surface up now
                        now everything epics now

∞

a few more minutes and we will have arrived

from the window the zones are obscured
by scratches on the screen: train railtracks
the path of the rail network and then fields
yes fields but the edge between fields
we could call this the fieldborder hedge
is too specific we mean something could
be green be railings not railtracks but fencing
and then in the fields zone against zones
the part where the fox looks up from the wheat
and the farmhouse at the top of the wheatfield
and the tracks and hedges but the rows and
the fox's bright ears up at the trainzone
and its eyes on the farmzone and the field
not the foxzone or later the horses at the top
by another edge of fencing or railing or hedging
and beyond that the townzone fabricated
pebbledash and the field cropped grass
and near the trainzone near me a dogwalker
with sheepdog the two in the fieldzone
and the demarcation of horsefieldzone
from dogwalkerfieldzone vying for space in space.
Nothing denies the grass and the speed
nothing my eyes dragged across this space
within which land rhymes with land and speed
with itself again because all these things are
exactly in themselves and nothing more.

Acknowledgements

The manuscript comprises extracts from two interwoven series, *from Animal Illicit* and *Fragments from an Imaginary Landscape*.

Earlier versions of parts *from Animal Illicit* have appeared in the following journals: '2/4/11 (unrecorded time)', '9/8/12 11:50-13:50' and 'At the Natural History Museum' in *The Clearing*; 'mutilated images' in *Futures: Poetry of the Greek Crisis*. 'earth is like earth falling' in *Rain of Poems*; 'feetfall' and 'a few more minutes and we will have arrived' in *Dandelion Jounal;* 'Something hurtling through the woods, which you try to record' and 'if I could just bring you back with love, then thought wouldn't be so painful' in *La questione Romantica: New Perspectives on William Wordsworth*; A Note on Process, 'This morning I saw a magpie', 'A circular walk', 'I am asking you if the birds' and 'i don't want to inflect' in *Stride*; 'for Maggie O'Sullivan' and 'Spider, Missing' in *Tears in the Fence*; 'Scientists no longer believe the green sea' in *Poetry Wales*; 'Bat' in *Under the Radar*; 'this year a delayed heat', 'if trees broadcast data', 'imagine / every name we share is precise', and 'Sussex Envoi' in *hotel*.

Selections from *Fragments from an Imaginary Landscape* have appeared in *amberflora, Tentacular, The Interpreter's House, Dandelion Journal, Wave Composition* (as 'In memory / Lee Harwood (June 6 1939 – July 26 2015)') and in a limited pamphlet edition produced by Smallminded Books (2016).

With thanks to the many wonderful editors labouring behind these magazines and books. Above all, thank you to Aaron Kent for shepherding these poems into book form.

Thanks also to the generous readers whose encouragement, time and support helped me organise and refashion these inherently disorganised and unfashionable poems—Zoë Brigley, Theo Chiotis, Simon Turner, Peter Blegvad, Rupert Loydell and Peter Riley. Above all, thank you to Florence Sunnen who reads my work even when it makes her very sad.

∞ ∞

LAY OUT YOUR UNREST

Lightning Source UK Ltd.
Milton Keynes UK
UKHW020808011020
370840UK00009B/283

9 781913 642273